Rappel

Rejoice For Rappel

"Rappel is not just a book; it's a testament to Joni's incredible journey and the wisdom she's gained along the way. Her words are infused with the same energy and passion that she brings to her clients whether in a consultation or a motivational speaking engagement. "Rappel" is a beacon of hope and a guide for anyone seeking to elevate their own life. As her mentor and friend, I am immensely proud of Joni's accomplishments. Her growth has been a source of inspiration for me, and I am confident that "Rappel" will inspire countless others to embark on their own journeys of self-discovery and empowerment. It is a gift to the world, and I am honored to have been a part of Joni's journey."

William Peel
Executive Director Mays Business School, Texas A&M University

"In Rappel: Break Through To A Better You, Joni Goodman offers readers a thoughtful and introspective journey toward self-discovery and personal growth. She guides readers through practical exercises designed to empower them to reach their full potential. This book is both a companion and a catalyst for becoming the best version of yourself. Congratulations, Joni, on writing such a meaningful and inspiring book."

Russell Richard
Senior Vice President, Center for Houston's Future

"Joni Goodman knows how to take motivation to the next level in her book, Rappel. Joni Provides insight on how to be the best version of yourself while being empowering, honest and an empathetic mentor. A must read book."

Kari Werner
President, Houston West Chamber of Commerce

"Rappel offers something rare: a rhythm for change that honors both emotion and forward motion. With a scientist's respect for structure and a humanist's heart, Joni Goodman gives readers the scaffolding they need to move through fear and into clarity—one week at a time."

Dr. Steffie Thomson
Founder & CEO, Steffie's

"Rappel: Break Through To A Better You is not just a book—it's an invitation. With raw honesty and inspiring clarity, Joni Goodman takes us to the edge of our own fears and gently challenges us to step into our discomfort zones, where true growth resides. Through powerful stories, reflective prompts, and stunning visual storytelling, this book becomes more than a guide—it becomes a trusted companion for those seeking courage, clarity, and meaningful transformation. Whether you're navigating a career crossroads or searching for deeper personal alignment, Rappel will meet you where you are and help you discover what's been waiting within all along. A bold and beautiful debut."

Kairy-tate Barkley
Owner, French Cuff Boutique

"Joni makes courage and clarity feel not just possible, but deeply personal."

Donna Hailey, MBA
Transformational Leadership Strategist

"Rappel is more than a book—it's a breakthrough companion. Joni Goodman beautifully blends personal vulnerability, neuroscience, and leadership wisdom to show that breakthrough doesn't always mean pushing forward—it sometimes means pausing, reflecting, and going deeper. With her 5Rs framework and authentic storytelling, she equips readers to face fear, reclaim their voice, and lead with clarity and courage. Joni's voice is bold, vulnerable, and deeply rooted in purpose. I see this being a trusted tool not just for personal growth, but for building stronger, more authentic teams and communities."

William Garay, Jr
Motivational Speaker, Coach, & Army Veteran

"Rappel is a powerful reflection of the authentic, courageous leader that Joni Goodman truly is. With heartfelt wisdom and practical insight, this book offers the essential tools we all need to achieve meaningful breakthroughs in our lives. Many of us long for transformation but struggle to find the way forward—Rappel provides a clear, actionable framework for living with authenticity and intention. Joni, who has been both a cherished mentor and a trusted friend to me, illuminates the path from fear to fearless. This indispensable resource empowers anyone ready to step into their full potential."

Stan Robbins
Leadership Consultant, Facilitator, & Coach

"Rappel is not just a book, it's a deeply personal guide into the layers of self-awareness, courage, and intentional growth. Joni Goodman's words invite readers to slow down and approach transformation with grounded honesty. Each breakthrough blends life experience with practical insight, offering a reflective space that feels both encouraging and real. Whether you're navigating change or simply ready to deepen your leadership, this book creates space for meaningful self-discovery, one mindful step at a time."

Rima Adil, Ed.D
Vice Chancellor, Houston Community College

"En un mundo que cambia a una velocidad vertiginosa y que muchas veces nos arrastra sin darnos cuenta, Rappel se presenta como una brújula poderosa para quienes desean mantenerse firmes en sus valores y fundamentos. A través de sus páginas, Joni ofrece una guía valiente y profunda para todos aquellos dispuestos a mirar hacia adentro y trabajar en sí mismos con radical honestidad. Desde su experiencia como coach, logra transmitir cercanía, como si caminara a tu lado en cada paso del proceso. Este libro me recordó una verdad fundamental como facilitador del cambio: no podemos ser agentes de transformación si no trabajamos día a día en transformarnos a nosotros mismos"

Arlette Grimaldo
Minerals IS Communication & Change Coordinator, Weir Minerals

"Joni has captured the essence of the hard work, personal dedication, and discipline to understand our vulnerabilities, emotional intelligence, and the courage to gain empathy and understanding of ourselves and those we love. Rappel is life-changing, and self-compassion is at its core. It takes grit and guts to dig deep, and thanks to Joni, she allows us to do so without judgment. Joni's fresh perspective is a gift to those who learn from her."

Constance White
Executive Director, Impact A Hero

"Rappel is like a gentle invitation to pause, look inward, and discover that true transformation often means going deeper rather than just climbing higher. Joni Goodman's heartfelt guidance and 5Rs framework offer a refreshing, compassionate path for anyone seeking clarity and authentic growth in both leadership and life."

Dr. Sravani Gullipalli
Technology Manager Services, Shell Lubricants

"As a technology consultant, I often face situations that require me to step outside my comfort zone, and this book provides practical tools to 'break through' and attract positive outcomes by shifting focus and mindset. I am grateful for that and for Joni's insights!"

Debbie Richards
International Keynote Speaker & Chief Technology Officer, Creative Interactive Ideas

"I was thrilled to learn that our Over The Edge event for Impact a Hero served as the inspiration behind Joni's powerful new book, Rappel: Break Through to a Better You. This thought-provoking work is more than just a book —it's a transformational tool for reflection, self-awareness, and personal growth. For anyone seeking to break through barriers in life or leadership, Joni's courageous descent offers a message that will undoubtedly elevate and empower those who choose to harness it."

Paul Griffith
Founder, Over The Edge Global

Rappel

Break Through To A Better You

Joni D. Goodman

Foreword By
Holly Hoffman

RAPPEL: Break Through To A Better You
Copyright © 2025 by Joni D. Goodman
All rights reserved.

Published by JDGAdvisors
www.jdgadvisors.com

ISBN (Paperback): 979-8-9991618-0-2
ISBN (eBook): 979-8-9991618-1-9

Book Editing by Sharon Nasr and William Peel
Book design by Angela Hoppe

For permissions, bulk purchases, media inquiries, or speaking engagements, please contact:
joni@jonidgoodman.com

First Edition
10 9 8 7 6 5 4 3 2 1

Dedication

To my late Aunt, Marilyn Bryan—a true breakthrough woman before the world had a word for it.

Your strength, conviction, and progressive spirit blazed trails within the FBI, the Indiana State Police, and IUOE Local 841 long before it was common or comfortable for women to lead in those spaces.

This book is for every leader who rappels into the unknown because someone like you made it possible.

Acknowledgements

Writing this book has been one of the most terrifying, humbling, and exhilarating journeys of my life, and I didn't take a single step without their support.

Armani, my partner, thank you for your steadfast support, encouragement, and understanding on the days when I was deep in writing mode or doubting myself. Your belief in me kept me anchored.

Gerti, my sweet fur baby companion, thank you for the quiet comfort, the tail wags, and the "Wisdom Walks" that brought clarity when I needed it most.

To my mom, Cathy, your strength through your breast cancer journey showed me what grace, grit, and faith look like in motion.

To my aunt, Marilyn Bryan, you were a true trailblazer! Your courage and leadership in roles in male-dominated fields inspired this book more than you'll ever know. Your legacy paved the way for women like me to lead with strength and grace.

To my dad, Kenny, thank you for showing me what it means to be steady while taking risks. Your encouragement gave me the confidence to keep going. "Might as well jump. Go ahead and jump." —"Jump" by Van Halen.

To my Nana, whose journey through pain and perseverance reminds me that breaking through often begins at the deepest point of resistance. Your heart is as big as your spirit is bold. Even when life dealt you barriers, you met them with beauty and resilience.

Sharon Nasr, your guidance, clarity, and magic behind the scenes made this book stronger than I could have imagined. Thank you for helping me say what I meant with heart and precision.

Bill Peel, thank you for championing my vision and encouraging me to dream bigger. Your guidance and perspective were a steady force in helping me shape this work.

Angela Hoppe and Team, you breathed life into this book with care, professionalism, and creativity. Your attention to every detail made the final result something I'm truly proud of.

Grace Perli, thank you for using your keen abilities to bring my vision to life. You create magic through your magnificence.

Carla Trusty-Smith, thank you for holding space with wisdom, compassion, and honesty. Your guidance helped me navigate the inner terrain required to write this book. I am deeply grateful for your presence on this journey.

Ann Pigue, thank you for always seeing me. Your wisdom and belief in my voice helped me find it when I needed it most.

Terry Braun, I appreciate you sharing your beautiful BiTerra ranch with me as a place of writing respite, where peacefulness and creativity flourished. Thank you for inviting me into your Texas family.

To my ATD Tribe, thank you for your ongoing support, encouraging a biochemist to align with her true north, writing, training, coaching, facilitation, and speaking.

To the EncounterYou™ Empresses, you are living proof that breakthroughs are real and possible. Your vulnerability, strength, and transformation gave this book its heartbeat.

To the Zumba Dancing Queens, you've been a source of joy, sweat, and sisterhood. Your energy reminds me to move, celebrate, and never take life too seriously.

To my WHIM SIM Mastermind, you are my compass and creative fire. Thank you for dreaming big with me, challenging me to rise, and holding space for the highest version of who I am becoming.

And **to the reader,** thank you for saying yes to yourself. Whether you're standing on the edge of something new or deep in the work, you are not alone. Keep breaking through to a better you.

With love and gratitude,

Foreword

FAITH. ATTITUDE. DETERMINATION. CONFIDENCE. DESIRE. PERSEVERANCE.

These six words have guided me through every challenge, on the island and in life—and they are the same six words that came to mind when I read "Rappel: Break Through To A Better You". Joni Goodman has written more than a book; she's given us a lifeline—one that reminds us how reflecting, relating, reasoning, recognizing, and rejoicing move us from fear to freedom.

I first met Joni in 2017 through the National Speakers Association, and from the start, I recognized a kindred spirit. We connected instantly over our mutual admiration for Survivor—the game that challenges not only your physical endurance but your mental and emotional strength. She shared the story with me of her breakthrough moment moving from biochemist to a master trainer, facilitator, and coach where she used the Survivor theme for her interview presentation and landed her first official role as a training specialist. As we shared stories and stages over the years, I witnessed the depth of Joni's heart, the power of her voice, and the intentional way she helps others find their breakthrough moment.

In Rappel, Joni takes us on a different kind of adventure—one that doesn't require an island, a camera crew, or tribal council. This is an inner expedition. A courageous descent into the stories, challenges, limiting beliefs, and big wins we all carry. With thought leadership, wisdom, and lived experience, she invites us to pause, reflect, and ultimately rise stronger.

Every breakthrough in this book is a moment of choice. A ledge you stand on. A rope you learn to trust. Whether you see yourself as a risk taker or someone who prefers the safety of the known, Joni's five-step framework will transform you. It will challenge you, stretch you, and strengthen the very core of who you are.

This book is more than inspiration—it's a transformational framework. It's a guide for leaders who are ready to move beyond performance and into purpose. For professionals who want more than success—they want significance. And for anyone who has ever stood on the edge of change wondering, "Can I really do this?"

Yes, you can.

I'm honored to call Joni my friend and even more honored to stand beside her as she shares this timely and transformative message with the world.

Now take a breath.

Trust and grab hold of the rope.
And rappel: break through to a better you.

Holly Hoffman, CSP
Survivor Finalist,
Professional Speaker, Author

Introduction

Have you ever done something that was both terrifying and exhilarating at the same time? Maybe it was launching a new business, delivering tough feedback to your team, taking a leap in your personal life, or stepping off the side of a 15-story building with nothing but a harness and a rope holding you.

That last one, rappelling? I've done it. And it changed everything in my life. What began as a give-back event to "Impact A Hero" (a veteran's non-profit) became the catalyst for one of the most profound revelations of my life.

What if the path to breakthrough wasn't up, but down? Life doesn't wait for you to be ready. It places you on the edge, urging you to leap. To descend. To pause. To reflect. To let go. And in doing so, you break through.

Whether you're a seasoned executive navigating complex change, a mid-career leader questioning what's next, or an entrepreneur staring down uncertainty, this book was written for you. We're all wedged somewhere between the risk-averse and the risk-taker. To be honest, most of us live in that middle space. We weigh decisions. Calculate. But deep down, we know that growth doesn't happen in our comfort zone. It's in that first daunting step into our discomfort zone—or that first leap!

A **breakthrough**, by definition, is:

breakthrough

[breyk-thro]
───────────

1.) A sudden change of situation.

2.) Making an important discovery that further advances you toward a goal.

3.) Achieved when barriers to current limitations are resolved.

It's not about perfection. It's about progression.

You don't need a helmet or harness to rappel. But you do need a willingness to step off the ledge of what you've always known to discover what's waiting below.

In Rappel: Break Through To A Better You, I lead you into a collection of breakthroughs that will challenge you to overcome fear, own your story, build meaningful connections, and lead with emotional intelligence and clarity. This is not a surface-level self-help book. It's a guide for those ready to transform not just how they work, but how they live.

You'll read breakthroughs—some personal, some professional— that reflect the internal and external moments we all face. You'll engage in reflective prompts called Breakthoughts designed to provide mindset focus and unlock momentum. While reading, you'll experience practical tools to break through whatever is holding you back.

The edge is right in front of you. Are you ready to break through?

How To Use This Book

Rappel: Break Through To A Better You is a tool for transformation—created with the intention of guiding you toward clarity, courage, and personal freedom. These breakthroughs are not meant to be rushed or consumed all at once. They are sacred moments of reflection. Choose to honor them at your own pace.

As a child, I was captivated by books with real-life illustrations and heartfelt stories. One of my all-time favorites, The Lonely Doll, is still one of my most prized childhood treasures. That book's illustrations left a lasting impression on me, and believe it or not, its style helped inspire the imagery in this book, which provides storytelling through photographs and emotion.

There are 52 breakthroughs within these pages, intentionally aligned with the number of weeks in a year. This is not a coincidence. If you so choose, take one breakthrough per week, allowing the message to marinate in your mind, body, and spirit. Sit with it. Journal about it. Speak it out loud. Answer the Breakthoughts reflection questions to begin the process of integration and momentum.

If you are in need of insight on a specific challenge—be it connection, leadership, confidence, emotional intelligence, or your next big step—go directly to that topic by using the Topical Index in the back of the book. The breakthroughs are meant to meet you exactly where you are.

As you move through the book, take time to notice the emperor butterfly hidden within each breakthrough image. The butterfly is a symbol of transformation and resilience emerging from stillness. It's a visual reminder that breakthroughs are sometimes hidden within, yet they are signs that something powerful is always unfolding beneath the surface.

This is your personal journey downward into truth and upward into strength. There is no right way or wrong way to rappel. There is only your way. Trust that wherever you begin, it is the right place.

Each breakthrough is a ledge. Each reflection a rope.
Descend deeper into who you truly are—
Rise with clarity into who you will become.
Break through to a better you!

Rappel

Sometimes life puts you on a steep cliff. It's a difficult choice to stay or leap. Rappelling is an exhilarating act of trust. With each controlled drop, you conquer your fears. The ropes become your lifeline, and the descent, your challenge. It's a dance between control and surrender, confidence and conviction.

Breakthoughts

What cliff do you need to rappel today?
How will you develop the courage to take the leap?

Own Who You Are

Own who you are. Embrace your true self with confidence recognizing that your brilliance and imperfections are what make you unique. Understanding these parts of you allows you to grow, lead, and thrive through self-acceptance and inner peace.

Breakthoughts

What strengths or imperfections do you need to fully own this week?

Share What You Discover

Connection through words, presence, and listening is the bedrock of your personal and professional life. Whether it's knowledge, insights, or personal experiences, share them all to inspire growth in others. By openly passing on what you learn, you foster connection, spark creativity, and contribute to a collaborative environment that benefits everyone.

Breakthoughts

How will you embrace boldness over familiarity and share your breakthroughs with those you value the most in your life?

Realize Your Full Potential

Your journey of self-discovery will steadily be guiding you toward the expansion of your current potential. With each step forward, you unlock new opportunities to learn, grow, and become the best version of yourself. The path may not always be easy, but it's a journey worth taking.

Breakthoughts

What action will you take today to move closer to realizing your fullest potential?

Feel It To Heal It

All emotions serve a purpose in our healing and well-being. Most of your transformation happens inside your pain. It happens in the valley—not at the mountaintop. The way to develop your resilience is to lean into the challenge, feel it, and find your wholeness, wisdom, and strength.

Breakthoughts

Remember a moment of pain.
Which emotion was the most difficult for you to feel and why? How did you address it?

Grow Stronger

Confront your obstacles and accept the growth that comes from facing your challenges directly. Endure, grapple with what feels difficult, and grow stronger. Remember, the only way out is always through. Each challenge is an opportunity for transformation.

Breakthoughts

How will you find meaning from your life challenges? Where can you use this knowledge to advance your life?

Attract What You Expect

The thoughts you focus on manifest in your life. When you focus on positive outcomes, habits, and experiences, you draw more positivity into your life. Make a conscious choice to focus on the positive and see your challenges as opportunities for growth.

Breakthoughts

Where is your focus?
What are you attracting and manifesting into your life?

Listen With Compassion

We have two eyes, two ears, and one mouth for a reason. You can express compassion to others by: noticing when they are uncomfortable, ensuring they feel safe and secure to express their feelings, talking less and listening more, and fostering a judgment-free environment. Connect with empathy and engage with compassion!

Breakthoughts

Under what circumstances will you begin to listen with compassion?

Appreciate Your Life

The law of attraction states that you simply cannot appreciate and celebrate wins without the contrast of challenges and disappointments of hard times. It's important to appreciate, learn, and grow from all the seasons in your life. There is magic in all the moments and growth occurs through every experience.

Breakthoughts

What has been one of your biggest lessons learned, thus far?
How did you grow from it?

Master The Art of Receiving Gratitude

Using gratitude as your north star, you will experience a life filled with more joy at home and in the workplace. Not only is it beneficial for you to give gratitude, but you must also be able to receive it.

Breakthoughts

How easily do you receive gratitude?
Where do you need to flex your gratitude receiving muscle?

Use Your Gifts

You have gifts that no one else in the world has to offer in the ways only you can. Your authenticity radiates naturally and is easily sensed by others. People can tell when you're not being true to yourself. Being authentic and transparent creates genuine connections and fosters mutual trust and respect.

Breakthoughts

What are the unique gifts you have to offer?
How do you demonstrate them authentically?

Believe In Abundance

Abundance is more than just a state of having—it's a mindset that requires daily commitment. Choosing to see possibilities, focusing on gratitude, and believing in limitless opportunities help attract prosperity into your life. It's a conscious choice you make every day, shaping your experiences.

Breakthoughts

How can you cultivate a mindset of abundance in your life today?

Step Into Your Discomfort Zone

Discomfort leads to growth. It pushes you beyond your limits, challenging your perspectives and abilities. You may not always feel good in the moment. When you stretch yourself and reflect on that experience, the result is growth!

Breakthoughts

What are three things you can do to stretch yourself? How will you inspire others to do the same?

W.A.I.T.
What Am I Telling Myself?

Every moment in your life is a new beginning with an opportunity to break through and become better than you were before. Your thoughts are as important as the food that nurtures your body. They can propel you towards your goals and growth.

Breakthoughts

How will you support a positive mindset using the W.A.I.T. affirmation?

EmbraceYou™

Expansion and growth occur whenever you are willing to take one step outside of your chrysalis of comfort. When you are introspective, presenting your most authentic self, embracing both your imperfections and potential, you are able to fully EmbraceYou™!

Breakthoughts

What are ways that you can garner support for your continued personal and professional growth?
How will you reciprocate?

Dance!

Take time to dance every day. Play your favorite music and move with expression. Dancing is more than just movement; it's a language of the soul. It allows you to express emotions words cannot capture. The rhythm of your body transcends barriers, bringing liberation and joy. Every step is an opportunity for exclamation and transformation.

Breakthoughts

Select your favorite song, turn up the volume, and dance to the music. How did it make you feel?

Connect With Empathy

The ability to establish empathy is one of the most essential leadership skills. Being empathetic offers you the ability to take the perspective of another while staying out of judgement and discussing the emotions that each is experiencing. Knowing how to be empathic will help you improve your connection with others.

Breakthoughts

Who do you need to extend more empathy to in your life? How? When?

Reflect What You Desire

Think of the law of attraction as the law of mirroring or reflection. Who you are inside is reflected in the people and situations you attract into your life. Based on this belief, everyone you meet is a mirror.

Breakthoughts

Who are the mirrors in your life and what do they show you?
How will you respond to them?

Recognize Your Worth

You are worthy of love, respect, and all the opportunities life has to offer. Your value is not defined by external achievements or the approval of others but by your inherent uniqueness and purpose. Embrace your worth, recognizing that you deserve every good thing that comes your way.

Breakthoughts

How do you start honoring your worth more deeply today?

Create Your Experience

You are the creator of your own experience, shaping your reality through your thoughts, actions, and decisions. Every moment offers the opportunity to choose how you respond to life's challenges. Your perspective, mindset, and belief system have the power to transform your world.

Breakthoughts

How will you take ownership of your current experiences and create the life you truly desire?

Reason to Relate

Reason to relate begins with the awareness that your attitude shapes your connections. When you choose to see others through a lens of empathy and appreciation, genuine relationships naturally form. By focusing on shared experiences rather than differences, you create space for understanding, trust, and meaningful connection. How you relate to the world—and the people in it—is a powerful choice, and it's one you can always control

Breakthoughts

How do you reason to relate in your life?

Know Your Value

In a world brimming with possibilities, it's important to recognize the value you bring to the table, both in your personal and professional pursuits. Discovering and embracing your worth is not a one-time action but rather a continuous journey of discovery and affirmation.

Breakthoughts

What intrinsic values do you contribute to those around you?
How do you manifest them in your daily life?

Assess To Become Aware

A breakthrough is a sudden change in a situation, such as making an important discovery, that rapidly propels you toward achieving a goal. Assessments are a fantastic way to gain insight into your strengths, tendencies, preferences, motivators, and emotional intelligence. If you have never experienced an assessment, do it.

Breakthoughts

Share any breakthroughs you have uncovered through personality or behavioral assessments.

Rejoice From Within

True happiness resides within you. It grows through self-acceptance, inner peace, and a sense of purpose. It's not dependent on external circumstances, but on cultivating a positive mindset and nurturing your inner well-being. Happiness results in moments of joy and celebration in your life.

Breakthoughts

What brings you the most happiness from the inside out?
What are some of your moments of joy?

Express Your Grief

Healthy grieving allows you to process your emotional pain in your own time. Grief is a natural response and by expressing your feelings, you release pent-up emotions. Through this process, you gain insights into yourself, foster resilience, and create space for growth. Avoiding grief can lead to emotional stagnation, while embracing it helps you heal and find meaning from the experience.

Breakthoughts

How do you healthily process grief?

Ignite Your Life

It's time to tap into the fullest expression of who you are. Rediscover the incredible person within you and recognize the potential you have to inspire and drive change. By making personal growth a priority, you unlock a plethora of new possibilities. You will discover the inner you and potential you never knew you had.

Breakthoughts

What actions will you take now to ignite your life passion and purpose?

Stand In Your Truth

See yourself embracing the transformative journey of self-discovery. Courageously break through the barriers that once held you back. Radiate an unwavering authenticity that enlightens you and others around you. Stand in your truth and invite the world to witness your fullest expression!

Breakthoughts

How will you align with your authentic self and create a lasting impact?

Add Color To Your World

Embrace your uniqueness. Your journey adds color to the world's canvas. Your voice sparks change and empowers minds. Your kindness ripples through hearts leaving a legacy of compassion. Your dreams inspire endless possibilities. Your beingness causes growth and expansion in both you and others.

Breakthoughts

In what ways will you celebrate your worth?
How will you add color to the world?

Become What You Respect

Surround yourself with motivated, inspiring, and confident people. Choose a mentor that adds value and meaning to your life. You need people in your life who empower you to continue to grow and develop your strengths, especially when times are tough.

Breakthoughts

Who is your mentor?
How does he/she embody the qualities you admire?
How do they influence your life decisions, actions, and values?

Engage Your Senses

You have five senses. Use all of them as many times a day as possible. They enhance your ability to open your mind and see what's possible. Light candles, play music, take mindful bites, write in your journal, and see your bright future. The blending of the senses accentuates your creativity.

Breakthoughts

What can you do today to engage your senses? How did it improve your experience?

61

Infuse Gratitude Into Your Life

It's easy to focus on what you want rather than what you have. However, when you shift your awareness to the present moment, you can be more intentional about finding moments of gratitude in your everyday life. Implementing practices like writing in a gratitude journal or filling up a gratitude jar activate this breakthrough.

Breakthoughts

How will you infuse gratitude into your daily life both giving and receiving?

Communicate With Intention

Communication is the foundation for all that we do personally and professionally. Notice how often there is an issue in your workplace or your personal life, that is due to miscommunication. Communicating with intention is being aware of your audience as well as the purpose and implication of your message.

Breakthoughts

Where and with whom will you be more intentional with communication in your life?

Choose You Now!

The most important decision you can make right now is to choose to invest in yourself. Your growth, well-being, and future depend on it. Whether it's through learning, self-care, or embracing new opportunities, this investment will pay off in ways that transform your life.

Breakthoughts

What is one action you will take today to focus on you?
How will you measure your success?

Name It To Claim It

Take this phrase to heart. It affirms your ability to identify and name your challenges, emotions, and growth opportunities. Claim them or accept them as your own and tame them by learning to fully exist amidst them. Ultimately overcome and transform them.

Breakthoughts

What are you claiming today?

Declare Your Value

You are enough. Your value is not defined by the opinions, expectations, or standards of others. You are important simply because you exist, with unique qualities that make you who you are. No one can diminish your inherent worth. You are always enough!

Breakthoughts

What steps will you take to begin owning your contributions?
How will you communicate your ideas?

Embrace An Attitude Of Gratitude

Adopting a gratitude-driven mindset transforms your relationships, enhances your work efficiency, and enriches your personal activities. It fosters positivity, improving both your interactions and overall well-being in every aspect of life. Embracing an attitude of gratitude will transform how you connect with others.

Breakthoughts

How will you embody this attitude of gratitude today?

Harness Your Inner Strength

You are a powerhouse, uniquely equipped with the strengths, talents, and resilience needed to achieve extraordinary results. Trust in your potential and know that you have everything within you to succeed. Every challenge is an opportunity to tap into that power.

Breakthoughts

What will you do to harness your inner strength and take action toward your goals?
Who is someone you will commit to sharing this with today?

Trust The Process

Sometimes life doesn't happen according to your timeline or expectations. You may face delays or setbacks. There will be passages that will be defining moments. Trust the process and understand that growth happens in both the highs and lows. Every circumstance, challenge, and milestone offers valuable lessons that contribute to your life experience.

Breakthoughts

How can you grow through your current challenges?

Take Action Now

The time is now to act toward your dreams and goals. Waiting for the "perfect moment" can lead to endless delays while today holds the potential for progress. Live in the present, trust your abilities, and step forward with confidence. The future is shaped by the choices you make and the actions you take today.

Breakthoughts

What can you start doing now to create the future you desire?

Mirror What You Admire

Reflect on the qualities you admire in others by adopting them into your behavior, creating a life that aligns with your values. Identify the areas you want to grow and expand in your life. Surround yourself with people who already possess these attributes. Mirror what you admire.

Breakthoughts

Which characteristics have you observed in others? How will you add them to your life?

Say "No"

When you say, "no" to something, you are saying, "yes" to something that better serves you and will ultimately be best for all involved. You can't truly invest in yourself if you are always giving your energy away to other people. Release the stigma and perception that saying "no" is not enough. "No" is a complete sentence. It's okay to say "no".

Breakthoughts

What is something you will say "no" to today?
How will that improve your life?

Invest In You

You are your own unique person and are exactly where you are meant to be right now. Cherish this awareness and the lessons you learn through your magnificent life experiences. Take time to give back to yourself. You can't pour from an empty cup.

Breakthoughts

How will you prioritize self-care to ensure you have the energy to support yourself and others?

Learn From Your Challenges

Learn through life's peaks and valleys, seeing every challenge and opportunity as a chance to grow. Let discomfort propel your personal and professional advancement, accepting it as a catalyst for growth and transformation. Step into your discomfort zone, knowing that growth lies there.

Breakthoughts

What steps will you take today to push you out of your chrysalis of comfort?

Manifest & Monetize All You Desire

Manifesting occurs when you free up space by acknowledging and releasing all limiting beliefs and inner barriers to your success. Monetizing happens when you pursue your passion without holding back. Manifesting and monetizing will only occur when you are showing up in your fullest expression and as your authentic self.

Breakthoughts

What do you need to manifest or monetize to break through to a better you?

Make Changes In Your Life

Don't let life pass you by too quickly. Take a stand to prioritize yourself by taking one step towards change daily. Document your progress. Celebrate the benefits of incremental improvement. Remember, the journey is a lifelong endeavor—a marathon, not a sprint.

Breakthoughts

What is one change you can make today that will have a lasting impact on your life?
How will you capture it?

Fill Your Own Cup First

Self-awareness isn't just a destination, it's a journey to nurture your own growth before you can overflow and give adequately to anyone else in your life. Prioritize pouring into your own cup first. This approach is not selfish, it's wholistic ensuring that you are showing up and sharing the best version of you.

Breakthoughts

What do you do to fill your own cup?
How do you share it with others?

Narrate Your Story

You are the victim and victor in your life's story, often shaped by circumstances beyond your control. The power is in your hands to claim the role of the narrator. You have the ability to write the next chapter of your life story. Do it with intention and purpose. Be bold and brave.

Breakthoughts

What narrative will you choose to write for yourself today?

Love Yourself

First, love yourself deeply and unconditionally. Embrace your strengths, acknowledge your flaws, and honor your unique journey. When you nurture your own well-being and practice self-compassion, you build the foundation for healthy relationships and success. Self-love empowers you to face challenges with confidence.

Breakthoughts

How can you show yourself more love and care in your daily life?

Maintain An Attitude Of Gratitude

Thankfulness can be temporary, often tied to specific events or moments, but true gratitude is a deep, enduring mindset. While thankfulness may come and go, gratitude remains constant, shaping how we view life, others, and ourselves. It is a powerful, lasting force that transforms experiences into meaningful reflections. Thankfulness is fleeting, but gratitude is longstanding.

Breakthoughts

What are you grateful for today?

Attract The Breakthroughs I Need

Albert Einstein says, "We can't solve problems at the same level of thinking that we used when we created them". To achieve a breakthrough, you need to operate with a growth mindset. A true breakthrough is an experience that feels extremely positive and requires transformation. You CAN break through to a better you.

Breakthoughts

What areas of your life do you most need to break through to a better you?

Create With The Universe

Align your inner dialogue with your deepest intentions. Ensure that your thoughts, words, and beliefs support your desires. When your mindset is in harmony with your goals, you create an energetic flow that attracts opportunities and success. Consciously nurture thoughts that reinforce the reality you wish to create.

Breakthoughts

What is the reality you wish to create for your life? How are you going to activate it?

EncounterYou™

Give yourself permission to be both brilliant and imperfect as you navigate your journey. Leverage your strengths while acknowledging areas for growth. This balance will enable you to take risks, learn from mistakes, and continue evolving. Grow through myriad experiences and boldly own who you are. Find your authenticity in all encounters.

Breakthoughts

When did you take a risk?
How did you use it to transform you?

Conclusion

You made it!

Throughout these pages, you've been invited to pause, reflect, and confront the patterns, inner barriers, and beliefs that may have held you back. You've done something powerful, you chose to show up for yourself. And in doing so, you've discovered that breakthrough doesn't always mean rising higher—it means going deeper. This is where true transformation begins.

Your journey doesn't end here.

The Rappel Framework was never meant to be linear. It's a way of moving through your life and leadership with greater clarity, presence, and courage. Whether you've just touched the surface or gone all in, this methodology will always be here to lead you to break through to a better you:

- **Reflect** – Own Your Story & Know Your Value
- **Relate** – Strengthen Emotional Intelligence & Build Meaningful Connections
- **Reason** – Cultivate Self-Trust & Use Discomfort as a Growth Catalyst
- **Recognize** – Gain Clarity & Take Purpose-Driven Action
- **Rejoice** – Celebrate Success & Share Your Story

Scan the QR code to receive support on your continued journey to break through to a better you!

Topical Index

Authenticity & Self-Worth

Discovering and owning your identity, value, and personal truth.

Emotional Intelligence & Inner Healing

Building awareness, resilience, and meaningful connection with self and others.

Growth Mindset & Personal Breakthrough

Shifting internal narratives and stepping boldly into transformation.

- **Facing Fear & Discomfort**
    - o Rappel – 3
    - o Step Into Your Discomfort Zone – 27
    - o Learn From Your Challenges – 87
- **Mental Reframing**
    - o W.A.I.T. (What Am I Telling Myself?) – 29
    - o Make Changes In Your Life – 91
    - o Trust The Process – 77
- **Forward Momentum**
    - o Ignite Your Life – 53
    - o Take Action Now – 79
    - o Choose You Now! – 67

Purpose & Vision

Aligning values with intention, creating impact, and living from the inside out.

- **Clarity & Direction**
    - o Realize Your Full Potential – 9
    - o Reflect What You Desire – 37
    - o Create Your Experience – 41
- **Manifestation & Alignment**
    - o Attract What You Expect – 15
    - o Attract The Breakthroughs I Need – 101
    - o Name It To Claim It – 69
    - o Create With The Universe – 103
    - o Manifest & Monetize All You Desire – 89

Gratitude & Abundance

Tapping into joy, fulfillment, and the richness of everyday life.

- **Gratitude as a Daily Practice**
  - Master The Art Of Receiving Gratitude – 21
  - Infuse Gratitude Into Your Life – 63
  - Embrace An Attitude Of Gratitude – 73
  - Maintain An Attitude Of Gratitude – 99
- **Appreciating Your Journey**
  - Appreciate Your Life – 19
  - Believe In Abundance – 25

Empowered Leadership & Influence

Leading with integrity, courage, and meaningful communication.

- **Leading from Within**
  - Use Your Gifts – 23
  - Grow Stronger – 13
  - Harness Your Inner Strength – 75
- **Communication & Connection**
  - Share What You Discover – 7
  - Communicate With Intention – 65
  - Become What You Respect – 59

Joy, Creativity, & Self-Expression

Living vibrantly, embracing play, and infusing life with meaning.

- **Creative Freedom**
  - Dance! – 33
  - Add Color To Your World – 57
- **Celebrating Self**
  - Engage Your Senses – 61
  - Mirror What You Admire – 81
  - Invest In You – 85

About The Author

Joni D. Goodman is a biochemist by trade turned experiential facilitator, master trainer, executive coach, and international speaker. Her superpower is cultivating safe spaces where leaders can let down their armor and authentically lead.

Originally from the small town, Linton, Indiana and now thriving in the big city of Houston, TX. Joni is the Founder & Chief Breakthrough Officer of JDGAdvisors where we are in the business of leading you to "Break Through To A Better You" through facilitation, development, coaching, and motivation.

Joni is the founder of the EncounterYou™ Luxury Women's Experience, her flagship program for women leaders in STEM. She is a sought-after speaker, facilitator, and coach, partner to Armani, and dog mom to a Miniature Poodle named, Gerti.

www.ingramcontent.com/pod-product-compliance
Lightning Source LLC
Chambersburg PA
CBRC090844120626
46551CB00011B/754